Prophetic Reflections

Other Books by the Author

The Last Kingdom Standing: Hope for a World in Crisis, Wipf & Stock, 2024

The Bridal Banquet: Holy Communion for House Churches and Small Groups, Wipf & Stock, 2025

Prophetic Reflections

A Living Apocrypha in Verse

Robert Schmidt

RESOURCE *Publications* · Eugene, Oregon

PROPHETIC REFLECTIONS
A Living Apocrypha in Verse

Resource Publications
An Imprint of Wipf and Stock Publishers
199 W. 8th Ave., Suite 3
Eugene, OR 97401

www.wipfandstock.com

PAPERBACK ISBN: 979-8-3852-7477-2
HARDCOVER ISBN: 979-8-3852-7478-9
EBOOK ISBN: 979-8-3852-7479-6

VERSION NUMBER 03/25/26

To the beloved memory of Karin
whose faith, life, and love
inspires hope for the future

The prophetic tasks of the church
are to tell the truth in a society that
lives in an illusion, grieve in a society that
practices denial and express hope in a
society that lives in despair

Water Brueggemann

Contents

Acknowledgments | ix
Introduction | xi

Chapter 1 God's Blessings | 1
Chapter 2 The Wrong Kingdom | 4
Chapter 3 The Great Denial | 7
Chapter 4 American Idolatry | 10
Chapter 5 Concerning Israel | 13
Chapter 6 About Russia | 16
Chapter 7 Challenge of China | 19
Chapter 8 The Challenge to Survive | 21
Chapter 9 The Law, Bent and Broken | 24
Chapter 10 Silencing Critics | 27
Chapter 11 Trembling in the Tumult | 30
Chapter 12 Civil Strife | 33
Chapter 13 Global Convulsion | 36
Chapter 14 A King of the Nations | 39
Chapter 15 A New World Society | 42
Chapter 16 Reconciliation of Enemies | 45
Chapter 17 Food for All | 48
Chapter 18 Water for the World | 51
Chapter 19 When Healing Is Free | 54

Chapter 20 Jobs and Housing | 57
Chapter 21 Freedom for Captives | 60
Chapter 22 Ending Wars | 63
Chapter 23 Forgiveness, Repentance and Forgiveness | 66
Chapter 24 The End of Death | 69
Chapter 25 Thy Kingdom Come | 71

Acknowledgments

I am indebted to sociologist Immanuel Wallerstein for his challenge to look beyond the present crises and propose new and innovative solutions to the problems we face. Walter Brueggemann revealed that the Hebrew prophets did just that in condemning the injustices of their time and rejoicing in the hope of a better future. His treatment of the grief over the tragedies in our world and the prophets' imagination of a radically different future is very moving. I also want to thank my daughter, Marian, whose willingness to help is inspiring, and my son, Michael, whose counsel and aid has made this work possible.

Introduction

If Isaiah and Jeremiah were alive today what would they say about America and the conflicts in our world? What would Amos say about the guiding goal of making America more prosperous? Of course they would say it in poetry. No words better combine moral outrage with the depth of compassion for a society gone wrong. The prophets spend little time on the stupidity and crimes of their kings. Rather they laid open, for all to see, the idolatry of a whole people who had lost their way. As Jeremiah spoke of the tragedies to come, he did it with tears in his eyes. Then to our amazement, every prophet also talks about the future so fantastic, so beautiful, only God could bring it about. Though coming in the future, the promises are based on some of the specifics of the past. Then as the evangelists are eager to tell us, Jesus forgives, feeds, and heals. He faces death head-on and wins the victory.

The word of the Lord in the Prophets and Evangelists is like a mirror in which we can see the reflection of what is happening in our world today. As the prophets, Mary, Simeon, and others, wrote in poetry, this is also a book written in a modern English rendition of Hebrew poetry. Like the prophets it addresses the sins of societies and kings, but it also lifts up the promises of God and how they might be realized. It is when we can envision a promising and exciting future that we can move from a tired despair to an energizing hope.

Like the Scriptures this little volume is arranged in short chapters and verses making it a living apocrypha. As in the Prophets, the poetry in each chapter is sometimes introduced by a statement of historical fact. In biblical fashion we have also identified each verse number with a number for reference. At the bottom of each chapter are references to biblical verses. As in similar references in many biblical versions, these are not always direct references but, in one way or the other, reflect one sense of the passage above. Though this book is presented in the form of a biblical layout, these verses, even those sections where God is pictured speaking, are in no way to be considered the word of God. They are merely an attempt to reflect what the prophets might say to our world today. In the past, literature of the Apocrypha was often introduced by saying that this has not been considered God's word as is found in the canonical Scriptures. Then they added, "But it is still good to read." Hopefully this living apocrypha might also still be good to read.

A wooden beam firmly bonded into a building is not loosened by an earthquake; so the mind firmly resolved after due reflection, will not be afraid in a crisis (Sirach 22:16).

Chapter 1

1The words of Robert, son of Walter and Gertrude, in the days of Trump in America, Netanyahu in Israel, Putin in Russia, and Xi in China. No special word of the Lord has come to me. No burning coal has touched my lips; I have not been invited to eat the script.
2Yet the word of the Lord in the Prophets and Evangelists is like a mirror in which we see a reflection of our own times. As a pastor and professor, called to speak the Word of the Lord from the Scriptures and apply it to this time, here are reflections of God speaking now to the people God loves.

God's Blessings

3Why does a mother love an errant child who hurts his playmates?
Why have I continued to bless the people of America? says the Lord.
4They built their nation on stolen land. Natives who were not killed were
rounded up, trekked afar, and poisoned with booze.
5Children were separated from parents, language, and love. Their unmarked graves
are testaments to false faith and frozen hearts.

6Why does a father bless his daughter named Liberty
when she enslaves a race and denies them the freedom to move and marry?

7Slaves picked the cotton. Their free labor helped to build mansions and fueled the Industrial Revolution.
8The backs of the slaves were marked by whips;
their grandchildren were hung by a noose.

9I loved and forgave by pure grace. The land brought forth undeserved riches.
My son laid down his life for their sin and soldiers died to free the slaves.
10Hope was reborn in the songs of the suffering. Jacob's ladder was one way up out
of a world of pain. They dreamt of going home.
11Pastor King marched for equal rights. Now all could eat where they chose, sit where they wanted, and vote for their candidate.
Yet many wait for worthwhile work and recognition of their creativity and resilience.

12Hear O heavens and listen all the earth. I made the people of America rich while
they killed the buffalo, dirtied my streams, and poisoned my air.
13They have mined my metals, pumped my black gold, cut down my trees, plowed my fields
but they boast of their prowess, their innovations and their efforts.
14Now the natives of the continent weep over its destruction and reverence what is left of its sacredness and beauty.
They are joined by all who seek inspiration and rest in my creation.

15I sent preachers who taught compassion. They warned of sin merged with might.
Powers were separated, rights enshrined, and justice practiced.
16Migrants came by the millions, welcomed to clear the land, and police the streets.
They forged the steel, built the roads, and taught the children.

17Wars were fought on distant lands. I provided peace from sea to shining sea.
I blessed you with wealth, safety, freedom, and the power to do good in the world.

18Millions were gifted to former enemies. Aid arrived to feed the starving, medicine for the sick.
American wealth was to be shared with a world in need.
19Peace Corps people volunteered to dig and teach, nurse and organize.
Trade was not always fair for our nation but brought hope and help for the struggling.
20What if a few immigrants, fleeing death, poverty and hopelessness, sneaked across the line?
They were greeted with thanks. They brought in the crops and cared for Dad at the home.

21Like Israel in the wilderness, there was murmuring in the crowd.
Even with full employment they complained, "We all want to be wealthy."
22It must be our ruler's fault; he gave the people too much money and prices rose a bit.
Yes, and there are too many refugees and immigrants, and they are criminals.
23Maybe if we elect the rich man, he will show how we can all get rich.
Secure in our wealth we can forget about the God of the dispossessed.

1:3 *Isa 1:2, Isa 2:7,* **1:4** *Hos 10:13,* **1:7** *Amos 5:11,* **1:9** *Isa 1:18 Jer 32:22,* **1:15** *Jer 3:15,* **1:21** *Num 11:1.*

Chapter 2

The Wrong Kingdom

1 A new white gospel spreads across the land. In the name of Jesus, it condemns the sins of other
people and promises prosperity for believers and contributors.
2 Of course it is for Americans. What is good for America is good for the world.
What the church cannot accomplish by teaching, its government should enforce by law.
3 For that we need a king to take our side and bless our condemnations. Who cares about his
morals as long as he can make our church's nation great again?

4 The prophets of corrupt kings have always done well. Silent about the nation's sins they were
aways generous in praising their monarchs.
5 But out of the cistern come the voices of my prophets. They cry out, "Save the refugees, shelter
the migrants, and welcome the prostitutes, some had abortions."
6 With my word they warn, unless this nation repents of its cruelty, its selfishness, its lust for
riches, and its disregard for a world in agony, it too will end in shame.

7Hear the word of the Lord: What is it to me that you have thousands for worship and can
broadcast to thousands more but cannot house the homeless?
8I do not delight in your praise bands, organ recitals, choirs, and festivals.
I am weary with your solemn assemblies, endless discussions, and meager charity.
9Even when you stretch out your hands and make many prayers,
I will hide my eyes from you and will not listen to you.

10They pray before they load their guns. Righteousness needs a militia for defense.
But Jesus refused his angel's legions. Was he just a loser on the cross?
11Who is their enemy? Those who tax so that the hungry might eat?
Those who vaccinate that the children might live?
12With camouflaged uniforms and night vision goggles they worship the wrong king.
My ears do not hear their prayer; my strength is made perfect in weakness.

13The Kingdom of God is at hand. You will be my church again. I have washed you with
my blood. Your sin is gone. None can find it; it has disappeared.
14The days are coming when the word of God is in the heart of every one of you.
I will commune with you and feed you with my love.
15Then you will walk with me to see the sick, visit the prisoner, welcome the stranger.
You will give water to the thirsty and work in the food bank feeding my people.

16Would you journey to far-off lands, see exotic sights, renew the
hope in your life?
Avoid the tourist ships, the great restaurants, and the crowded
galleries.
17Visit Kakuma Camp in Kenya, the slums of Mumbai, and Africa's
rural clinics.
Walk with the archbishop to visit the poor in Buenos Aires.
18The Kingdom comes to all the earth. No power can hold it back;
no crime can stop it.
Death has lost its sting. Kingdom folk live forever.

2:1 *Acts 19:13*, **2:4** *Jer 28:1–2*, **2:5** *Jer 38:6, Matt 21:31*, **2:6** *Amos 4:1–2*, **2:8** *Isa 1:11–14*, **2:10** *Jer 14:14*, **2:13** *1 Cor 6:9–11*, **2:14** *Jer 31:33*, **2:18** *Dan 2:44, 1 Cor 15:55, Rom 8:37–38.*

Chapter 3

The Great Denial

1Americans voted for Trump though he promised to ignore climate change. Again in 2025 he pulled out of the Paris Climate Accords supported by over 100 nations across the world. Not only did he deny that climate change was caused by human activity but sought to abolish agencies dealing with climate change and reject all reference to climate change in his administration.

2Would the cow destroy her pasture, the bear his forest, the salmon
their seas?
But my people are burning their air and boiling their waters.
3Have they not learned, are they too blind to see? The land needs
a sabbath.
Harvest just enough and be satisfied with the manna for today.
4Now howling winds destroy; forests and homes are torched,
it is hard to breathe in Delhi's streets and Mexico City's
markets.

5Cows and goats die and dry in the fields that are growing deserts.
Their shepherds travel over sage and seas for shelter and safety.
6Floodwaters wash away the lives of sleeping children.
Who will wipe away their mother's tears?
7Forest fires burn hotter now and flames reach the clouds.
Their smoke makes it hard to breathe even in pleasant places.

8Where are the prophets who warn of trouble and tell of disaster?
Forbidden to speak, only the courageous will scream.
9It is my world that the wealthy destroy, squeezing out its life for gain.
Trash fills the fruitful valleys; plastics poison the widest seas.
10Have you no eyes to see the beauty of my land fading from view?
Have you no ears to hear death wails of the wild ones?

11Yet the days are coming, says the Lord who created all.
Streams will flow in the desert bringing life and hope.
12Flowers will bloom in the rocks and sand.
Green grasses will bring new life to the hungry.
13The sun will bring water from the seas and the power of the wind
will water the land and harvest its bounty.

14My trees will lift up your eyes to their maker and yours.
My mountains will be an altar for your worship.
15The beauty of my creation shines forth through the life of my Son.
His love inspires and recreates all life and hope.
16His sacrifice forgives the sins against our world.
His frugal life shows us how to live.

17Are these the last days? How soon will it end?
Plant a tree today and water the tired flower.
18Birth the babes and raise them up to plant a garden.
Keep the memory of Eden alive in all the rows.
19Fence off the forest to house my fawns and cubs.
Stretch out the savanna for my zebras and cheetahs.

20Protect the seas that praise the Lord and cherish the snows and rains.
Esteem the lakes and all hills that reflect his beauty.
21Fruit trees and all cedars bow down to thank their maker.
Beasts of the wild and cattle of the field bend their heads in prayer.

22Let all the rulers on earth praise the Lord of all creation.
Help them reverence all that God has made.

3:3 *Lev 25:3, Exod 16:16–21,* **3:5** *Joel 1: 17–20,* **3:8** *Isa 30:10,* **3:11** *Isa 35:6,* **3:12** *Isa 51:3* **3:15** *John 1:4,* **3:16** *John 3:16, Luke 9:58,* **3:19** *Isa 65:25,* **3:20–21** *Ps 148:7–11.*

Chapter 4

American Idolatry

1 Prosperity, your name is Ba'al. Come worship him with sin and sacrifice.
Your president is his high priest; your stock markets are his temple.
2 Why have my people left the congregations that championed the refugees and homeless?
They flock to those that are doing well with Ba'al's blessings.
3 You have forsaken the God who brought you out of hunger and conflict.
Who blew the wind that sailed the ships that landed you here?

4 An incurable disease has seized the minds of many deluded by Ba'al.
Madness makes them chase the wealth they can never spend.
5 They will choke on the all goods they cannot swallow.
Garages are full of rubbish that will never be used.
6 They do not judge with justice the refugees they deport.
They do not defend the rights of the vulnerable and needy.

7 The idols of Ba'al are worshipped as bullish markets and beautiful mansions.
Advertising evangelizes and seduces the unwary for happiness.

8Without shame, lust is loosed to sell perfumes and performances.
Marriages are forsaken in exchange for Asherah's erotic promise.
9Why have you left the God who made you for all that perishes?
Idols made with hands have never had the power to bless and save.

10Who can count the wealth of our rulers who exploit the desire to become rich?
Who can afford to build houses for people sleeping on the street?
11Who will support the schools that feed the children of the poor?
Who will pay the teachers who have bigger classes and less help?
12The wives of the wealthy want still more to display their worth.
The nakedness of their pretension is visible to all.

13Your bag of coins is torn; your treasure chest will empty soon.
No one will have the money to buy your goods, floods and fire will finish your homes.
14Do not depend on Europe; Canada and Mexico are not your friends.
Standing alone, a new world order surrounds you.
15Your righteousness is gone; respect for your values has vanished.
Wolves are waiting in the wings for you to perish.

16Like the rich man with flocks of sheep too many to count
you desire the lamb of the neighbor who has only one to hold.
17With tariffs to add more sheep to your flock to make you wealthier still
you steal the jobs of African mothers and rob workers in Canada and Mexico.
18To excuse your theft, you tell of American workers who have lost their jobs.
You did little to help them then and just pretend to help them now.

19But the days are coming when Zaccheus gives his money back.
Matthew leaves his graft; and Joseph gifts a tomb.
20Then everyone will sit under their own vine and fig tree.
Now the workers, not the state, will own the firm.
21Refugees, without fear, will be secure in their own homes.
Their children will laugh and play with pets.

4:1 *Jer 7:9*, **4:3** *Hos 2:8*, **4:6** *Isa 10:1*, *Jer 5:28*, **4:8** *2 Kgs 21:7*, *Hos 4:14*, **4:9** *Isa 57:13*, *Jer 10:5*, **4:10, 11** *Jer 5:28*, **4:12** *Amos 4:1–3*, **4:16** *2 Sam 12:7*, **4:19** *Luke 19:8*, *Matt 9:9*, *Matt 27:57*, **4:20** *Zech 3:10*.

Chapter 5

Concerning Israel

1From the slave markets of Egypt, I brought my Israel to the promised land, says the Lord.
Babylon and Persia could not keep you; I brought you home again.
2Scattered everywhere you were persecuted and oppressed, murdered by the millions.
I wept for your torment; who could forget your anguish? I brought you home again.
3I invited you to be the faithful stewards of my land;
I have led you home again that my righteousness might be a beacon of hope.

4Your sages called for sharing the land with Ishmael's children.
Arabs are good shepherds and nurture the olive groves.
5But you worshipped the might of Joab; only battle can bring victory.
Like Joab, you kill the innocent and David's curse will find you.
6You locked them up in Gaza and were surprised when they wanted out.
They copied the way you killed their fathers; like you, they took hostages.

7You wear the Holocaust like a glorious white garment.
It pardons bombing the hospitals and schools.
8The body bags of women and children cover the streets.
More are buried under their bedroom's rubble.
9Beware of the weeping of the mothers, the starvation of the children.
They ignite the world's wrath and the end of my favor.

10With borrowed bombs you have blasted enemies.
Hezbollah is hurt; Iran's generals are assassinated.
11Refugee camps lie in ruins; their children are now in prison.
Your new houses are built on stolen land and wasted olives.
12Netanyahu glories in his army's might and drone's success.
But I hear the cries of his victims and will never forget.

13"It is our land," the settlers cry; "God has promised it to us."
Then why did God bless Assyria and Babylon to take it?
14We came back to Jerusalem; now it is ours again.
But why did Tiberius scatter you around the globe?
15The whole land will soon be ours; God's promises will be fulfilled.
Will God take it from you again?

16For three transgressions of Edom and for four I will not revoke the punishment.
He pursued his brother with a sword and cast off all pity.
17For three transgressions of the Ammonites and for four I will not revoke the punishment.
They ripped open pregnant women to enlarge their territory.
18For three transgressions of Israel and for four I will not revoke the punishment.
They bombed my women and starved my children so that they can never vote in my land.

[19]The Zionist dream is buried in the burned Kibbutz, the hostages,
and the soldiers lost in war.
Jews are safer in America and Germany.
[20]Why do you copy the Nazis that starved the children in the
camps?
Their cruelty never destroyed the Jewish people.
[21]Will the remnant of Gaza someday build a museum
recounting the inhumanity of their own Holocaust?

[22]Again, I will make Jerusalem my city of peace.
Love will replace anger; mercy will quell revenge.
[23]The children of Abraham will play together.
In their little lives I will house my temple.
[24]No longer will Jerusalem kill the prophets sent to it.
Their visions of peace and plenty will be fulfilled.

5:1 *Ps 81:10, 1 Chron 36:33,* **5:3** *Exod 19:5,* **5:5** *2 Sam 3:27–29,* **5:9** *Jer 31:8,* **5:12** *Amos 8:7,* **5:13** *Exod 3:17, Isa 8:7,* **5:14** *Luke 19:43, 44,* **5:16** *Amos 1:11,* **5:17** *Amos 1:13,* **5:18** *Amos 2:6, 7,* **5:22** *Ps 122:6, Isa 52:9.*

Chapter 6

About Russia

1Threatened by a freer, independent nation next door, Russia in-
vaded Ukraine. After early defeats it mobilized the resources of
is vast territory and mustered thousands to be sacrificed in the
conflict. Unable to achieve a quick conquest it has sought vic-
tory through bombardment and endless incursions. 2Deterred by
Ukraine's army and weapons from abroad, it has enlisted support
from China, North Korea, and Iran and with them are seeking a
new world order. As it continues the conflict, has a new world war
begun?

3The dream of Russia to be the Third Rome is in tatters.
    All that is left are the empty lots filled with rusty cannons.
4But dreams die hard; "Oh to be imperial Assyria!"
    They were feared and respected by the world.
5 With the blessing of the church our Sargon subdues small nations.
    He brings to Russia all the children he has captured.

6As Assyria laid waste to Ammon, Moad, Edom, Syria and Israel,
    you bombed Chechnya, defeated Georgia, subverted Moldova, and invaded Ukraine.
7Your victims are children in orphanages, civilians shot in the streets;
    every night the sky rains down fire and death.

8 Millions have fled the war to seek safety from the savagery.
Thousands lie in graves leaving a grief that does not go away.

9 Your people are quiet when the nation seeks greatness through war.
That has long been the secret of every emperor's success.
10 Russia's greatest power has been the patience of its people to suffer;
Putin makes them proud when they bury their sons lost in war.
11 He creates an enemy who might do them harm.
Then most will be satisfied with their poverty and want.

12 Stalin turned Communism into a façade for conquest.
Putin uses faith to rob the nation of its wealth.
13 Who owns the oil fields, the refineries, the timber, and the caviar?
Once the property of the state, it now pays for yachts and villas.
14 Can faith in Mother Russia still be used for the conquest of Ukraine?
Will Lithuania's children be next in Putin's march to the sea?

15 Has Russia lit the fuse to bring the world to war?
Europe increases in armed forces day by day.
16 Iran supplies drones; China contributes technology;
Kim Jong Un sends artillery shells and men to die in Ukraine.
17 No longer just for Defense, the US now has a War Department.
With joy it sells weapons of death to the world.

18 Who will invade Russia when my snows protect your heartland?
The next invasion will come from within, by those angered by the theft and slaughter.
19 Not all will be killed in prison and flying on your planes;
a remnant will grow to pierce your posture and pretense.

20The true greatness of Russia will be shown in the art of those who
have suffered.
My strength is always made perfect in weakness.

21My monks gave you the power to write.
I saved you twice from powers greater than yours.
22Rebuilt churches will dot the country with blessings.
My birds will sing hymns in your birches.
23May your prophets of peace be living icons for the faithful.
I will help you beat your swords into plowshares.

6:4 *Isa 8:7,* **6:5** *Isa 20:1,* **6:6** *Isa 15–19,* **6:7** *2 Chron 36:17,* **6:14** *Lam 2:19,* **6:18** *Jer 50:2,* **6:19** *Jer 50:18,* **6:20** *2 Cor 12:9,* **6:23** *Isa 2:4.*

Chapter 7

Challenge of China

1With clouded vision he sees the finger of a hand, writing on the
wall
MENE MENE TEKEL PARSIN
2Who will interpret it? Why is the emperor pale with fear?
Will the prophet of God tell us what it really means?
3Because of your haughty pride, God has numbered the days of
your kingdom.
Your land is divided; the Medes and Persians will take it.

4With America polarized, will China be the Medes and Persians?
Once poor and oppressed, how could China be a threat?
5Meager soil, filched technology, and misguided revolution,
how could it compete with real wealth and might?
6Have you not seen as it grows in its greatness
"It is I, the Lord, who will use it for my purpose," says the Lord.

7Who will lead the world in the next hundred years?
Who will stop using fossil fuels for energy?
8What nation of the North builds roads and bridges in the South?
Africans now sell cassava and yams across a river.
9Who will buy the soybeans of farmers in Argentina and Brazil?
Now they can buy the electric cars that China makes.

[10]While America cuts funds for scientific research,
China advances learning for technological progress.
[11]With coal-dark days, China works to cut down emissions.
With smoke-filled skies, America denies climate change.
[12]It was I who blessed China's rise from poverty to plenty, says the Lord;
Shall I not punish Belteshazzar for his false gods?

[13]But why arouse the bruised tiger by invading your nearby neighbor?
Is your pride more important than the welfare of your millions?
[14]Why provoke a war over oiled islands in the sea?
Let wind and sun continue to power your progress.
[15]Why enslave the Uyghurs and limit the liberties of your people?
I hear their cries and will give them strength to endure.

[16]With Mao you banned the missionaries and buried their churches,
but the seeds they planted are blooming all around.
[17]Churches are being built, and sermons are being spoken.
Some on bicycles ride forty miles to hear them.
[18]Gathering into houses, thousands of the faithful listen and pray.
Spilling out they serve the disabled and help the weak

[19]Do I not cause empires to rise and to fall?
All glories of Babylon and the Medes and Persians are gone.
[20]But I have a Kingdom that will last forever.
Though hidden, no one can take it from me.
[21]Scattered like seed it grows in every land.
Like the mustard tree, it invites the birds to rest.

7:1 *Dan 5:25*, **7:2** *Dan 5:6*, **7:3** *Dan 5:28*,**7:6** *Jer 25:8*, **7:12** *Isa 43:14*, **7:15** *Exod 22:27*, **7:16** *Matt 13:8*, **7:19** *Dan 2:21*, *Ps 135:10*, **7:20** *Dan 2:24*, **7:21** *Matt 13:32*.

Chapter 8

The Challenge to Survive

1Who seeks to purchase and control the way we live our lives?
The prophets of Ba'al have taken over Ahab's Kingdom.
2Weather threatens their profits as they must pay for the drought.
Margins shrink as they compete over smaller markets.
3Let us purchase governments across the world to guarantee our wealth;
we will pay for culture wars and people will elect Ba'al's bullies.

4Go tell King Ahab that Elijah is here, said a fearful Obadiah.
After serving the poor, God's prophet confronts the king.
5Let there be a contest between the God of all and the prophets of Ba'al.
Who will end hunger, poverty, disease, and war?
6Unafraid, Ba'al's prophets pointed to their wealth and hoped it would spread.
They prayed to Ba'al, cut themselves, and nothing happened.

7Debts continue to rise in the poor nations of the world;
there is not enough money to pay for the clinics and medicines.
8Well-paying jobs for the thousands of school leavers do not exist.
Without hope some join gangs, others fight for a forged faith.
9Despair breeds anger and rage leads to conflict.
How can the prophets of Ba'al deal with failed states?

10Slum dwellers sell trinkets and peanuts to the passerby.
Sometimes hunger makes their lives so hard.
11As hope grows dim they seek a way to wealthy lands;
with a job they can send home money to their mom.
12"But they cannot stay here," the wealthy say.
"First we lock them up and then will send them back."

13Elijah watches as the prophets of Ba'al cannot compete;
with prayer he builds my altar for a harder task.
14The flames of my spirit quicken warmth in chilly hearts.
Churches take collections, missionaries move mountains.
15U.N. trucks of food flood the camps of refugees and their children;
money is pledged to end the misery and malaria.

16Greater than the power of kings, richer than the reserves of the wealthy,
is my power to move the hearts of my people throughout the world.
17Mothers sacrifice their lives for their children;
fathers struggle and strive to feed their families.
18People gather to protest the cruelty of CEOs and kings.
I provide the patience and perseverance for them to win.

19The prophets of Ba'al are condemned by the words of my Son,
"You cannot serve God and wealth."
20"It is easier for a camel to go through the eye of a needle
than for a rich man to enter the Kingdom of God."
21To a rich man he said, "Sell what you have; give money to the poor,
and you will have treasure in heaven. Follow me."

22Jezebel, Ahab's wife and Ba'al's champion, is livid with rage.
Who can survive the wrath of wealth merged with power?
23Elijah flees to the mountain of God and waits in despair.
What can a single person do in the face of tyranny?

[24]I did not answer with world-shaking events, but in a still small voice.
You still have work to do, and you are not alone, says the Lord.

[25]Do not be surprised that you live in a land with a bad king and court.
There my prophets lived and suffered and sometimes died.
[26]But their deeds and words have a life that outlasts their despots.
They bring us courage and hope in the face of evil.
[27]Challenge the prophets of Ba'al and their protectors to a contest!
Whose god can best help the vulnerable and needy?

8:1 *1 Kgs 16:32*, **8:4** *1 Kgs 18:8*, **8:5** *1 Kgs 18:19–24*, **8:13** *1 Kgs 18:32*, **8:16** *Acts 4:34*, **8:19** *Luke 16:13*, **8:20** *Mark 10:35*, **8:21** *Matt 19:21*, **8:22** *1 Kgs 19:2*, **8:23** *1 Kgs 19:8*, **8:24** *1 Kgs 19:18*.

Chapter 9

The Law, Bent and Broken

1 After his election in 2024 President Trump insisted that all refu-
gees and immigrants who came into the country illegally could be
deported because they broke the law on entry into the country.
As a result, thousands have been deported for no other reason.
Yet, he freed over a thousand who broke the law when they rioted
to overthrow an election. 2 Upon taking office, he forced law firms
to provide him with free legal services for causes he supports. In
these efforts he has joined with other authoritarian rulers in bend-
ing and breaking the rule of law.

3 Happy are those who do not follow the advice of the wicked, or
walk in the path of sinners,
but their delight is in the law of the Lord, and on his law they
meditate day and night.
4 The laws of God and men are decrees and precepts for justice in
the land.
They are commandments to treat our neighbor fairly and all
people with equity.
5 When laws are bent and broken, rulers judge unjustly and are
partial to the wicked;
victims are the weak and orphan, the lowly and the destitute.

6Wearing masks and carrying guns they roam the parking lots for strangers.
They look for fathers and husbands who will not come home tonight.
7It makes no sense for those who depend upon their labor and sell them surplus goods.
But here is a quota that must be filled, promises that must be kept.
8The law does not support their capture, detention, and deportation without a trial.
But laws are waived when they serve not whims of the wicked.

9Black fathers talk to sons about how to survive injustice on the streets.
Show your hands, obey every command, and don't get shot.
10The law presumes all to be innocent; all are equal before the law.
Why then does a colored skin presume guilt of something or the other?
11Why are so many black faces in prison cells across the nation?
Is that the way the law was written or the way the law is enforced?

12The nation was built on the rule of law; its foundation is the Constitution.
Judges were not to be partial to the rich, the poor, or the party.
13But courts favorable to the president decide the cases he champions.
He scolds and derides the judges who disagree with his desires.
14With threats to exclude law firms from the halls of government,
the president receives free legal services while opponents face financial disaster.

15The law is twisted inside out when nation's lawyers are directed to prosecute political foes;
hatred-based retribution is replacing the prosecution of crimes.

16 Justice is turned back, truth stumbles in the public square, and uprightness cannot enter,
Truth is lacking and whoever turns from evil to do right is dishonored,
17 Impartial observance of the law is moving away from us; righteousness eludes us,
We wait for light and lo, there is darkness, for brightness, but we walk in gloom.

18 We wait for the justice of God: a bruised reed he will not break and a dimly burning wick he will not quench.
19 The Lord supports the cause of the needy and executes justice for the poor.
The righteous will give thanks to your name and will delight in your presence.
20 The days are coming when I, the Lord, will raise up a good king who shall rule wisely.
He shall execute justice and righteousness across the whole land.

9:3 *Ps 1–2*, **9:5** *Ps 82:2–3*, **9:13** *Isa 59:14–15*, **9:16** *Isa 59:14*, **9:17** *Isa 59:9*, **9:18** *Isa 42:3*, **9:19** *Ps 140:12*, **9:20** *Jer. 23:5*.

Chapter 10

Silencing Critics

[1]Students and faculty of major universities have been critical of US policies in the Middle East. They have also opposed the administration's prohibition of diverse, equitable and inclusive policies (DEI) as a way of benefitting minorities. [2]To silence these critics the administration has threatened universities by limiting government funding, restricting international students, and taxing their endowments and non-profit status. [3]The government has also filed lawsuits against media networks they believe are critical of the president's policies. [4]They have also tried to silence comics poking fun at the president and his policies. Even past critics cannot escape as lawsuits are filed against officials the president believes to be his enemies.

[5]A babbler who is rebuked will only hate you;
the wise, when rebuked, will love you.
[6]When the prophet, Nathan, accused the King of stealing a poor man's sheep,
David repented of having an innocent man killed.
[7]When Jeremiah warned the King of the coming disaster of the nation
the prophet was punished and put into a pit.

8 Critics of rulers are caught in the crosshairs of the coming convulsion.
They must choose between their commitment to two kings.
9 With the power to silence, pursue the lawsuit and swing the sword,
the nation's king can cower his most concerned critics.
10 Yet, God, the mightier King, has established the world of many nations.
He is the ruler of righteousness, lover of justice, and promoter of equality.

11 False prophets owe their allegiance to the nation's king and can win his favor.
Critics of the nation and its rulers are often resisted and ruined.
12 But kings die, nations will be defeated, and all their glory is dishonored.
Important for just a little while, the king's court of counselors will soon be over.
13 With divine compassion I will lower the ropes and lift the prophets from the pits.
I will inscribe their words on living parchments which can be read by all, says the Lord.

14 Not all critics of kings and their counselors are the prophets of the most high God.
Many champion causes and concerns that benefit other peoples' pride and pocketbooks.
15 Are the apples small and wormy? Have they fallen off the tree too soon?
Is it a good tree? By their fruits you will know them.
16 Praise the critics who love God's creatures, who would help the vulnerable.
They speak for peace, protect our world, and show kindness to the stranger.

[17]In the worst of times a promise was revealed to bring light to the world:
I will raise up a King who will deal wisely and execute justice.
[18]Here is my servant, whom I have chosen, my beloved with whom my soul is pleased.
I will put my Spirit in him, and he will proclaim justice to the Gentiles.
[19]He will not cry out loud or make his voice heard in the street.
He will not break a bruised reed or quench a smoldering wick until he brings justice to victory.

10:5 *Prov 9:8,* **10:6** *2 Sam 12:3,* **10:7** *Jer 38:5–6,* **10:10** *Ps 99:4,* **10:11** *Amos 7:10–12,* **10:13** *Jer 38:13,* **10:15** *Matt 7:19–20,* **10:17** *Isa 32:1,* **10:18, 19:** *Isa 42:1–3.*

Chapter 11

Trembling in the Tumult

1Fear not when the world changes and the mountains tremble,
though the waters foam and the earth melts.
2Iraq could not pretend to be a great power and conquer Kuwait.
Iran could not defy the wealthiest nations to seek respect.
3Africa's millions could not even pretend to challenge their exploiters.
How long will the poor in Latin America have to wait?

4They have come by the thousands, crossings on boats to Italy, and France;
Greece is overwhelmed; Hungary has locked the doors.
5The British do not know what to do about the rubber boats coming across the Channel;
migrants fuel Germany's frightening alternative opposition.
6The United States builds a wall and sends troops to defend the border.
Masked men with bulletproof vests arrest and deport those who have come.

7Migrants and refugees are a sign that the world's economy does not work for the poor.
Out of work people fight the wars that ravage failed states.

8On their phones they see the wealthy boarding cruise ships for traveling in comfort.
Migrants work hard hours to afford rice and beans in a real home.
9Now the strife between rich and poor is not fought behind the barricades
but in courthouses where asylum seekers come to plead their case.

10A tsunami is about to wash over the whole world; its waters roar and foam.
The mountains tremble with its tumult.
11Global communications, technology, climate change, immigrants, and trade
are invading every land, tribe, religion, city, culture, and family.
12The waters threaten to submerge the values on which we built our lives.
Mosques and Hindu temples live in Christian cities.

13Jobs have been exported around the world, and cars are imported from abroad;
will migrants and refugees take our jobs and flood our schools?
14"We do not believe those who warn of the earth getting warmer.
Are vaccines and science simply scams to limit our freedom?
15Can we build a dike to keep the waters away, sandbags in front of our door?
Let us join our fears and pride . . . and hope it will all go away."

16"We need a leader who will defend us and our culture against a marauding world.
We will support Putin against the invasion of the delights of Europe.
17Xi can be counted on to put China first and resist the foreign notion of individual liberty.
This is a time for national pride to resist the invasion of foreign faiths.

[18]Americans champion a president who will put America first.
He praises the culture of the people and protects the wealth of the rich."

[19]Why do the nations conspire together, and the people plot against me? asks the Lord.
Why do the rulers take counsel against the Lord and his anointed one?
[20]It was I who led the empires to swallow up Moab, Syria, Israel and Judah.
National pride and power could not to save them from death and exile.
[21]Am I not behind the changes sweeping our world, threatening our peace?
Instead of fears for the future, it is time for true repentance.

11:1 *Ps 46:23*, **11:4** *Ruth 1:1*, **11:7** *Ps 37:14–15*, **11:9** *Ps 119:154–55*, **11:10** *Isa 17:12*, **11:12** *Jer 46:8–9*, **11:15** *Lam 2:14*, **11:19** *Ps 2:1–2*, **11:20** *Isa 1:27*, **11:21** *Isa 7:5–7*.

Chapter 12

Civil Strife

1 In the United States National Guard troops and US Marines were
sent to Los Angeles to protect facilities used to detain captured
refugees and migrants, some of whom had come to the country
illegally. 2 Other troops were sent to Washington, DC, Memphis,
Chicago, and Portland with threats of more to come. Most were
greeted by massive protests and defiance from local officials.

3 O Lord, as we look to our nation we see trouble and wrongdoings.
Destruction and violence are before us; strife and contention are all around.
4 The war between the global invasion and the pride of our nation has begun.
Refugees are handcuffed before being thrown into vans and carried away.
5 Like the speck in the eye the foreign substance must be removed
but it is hard to see from behind the log that blocks our view.

6 Opponents are condemned, revenge is tolerated, and politicians are targeted.
Friendly disagreements seem like a memory of the past.
7 Hateful speech spreads from political rallies to university forums.
Anger festers, passions are aroused, a political activist is murdered.

8Remember, O Lord, what has happened to us; look to see our disgrace.
But you, O Lord, reign forever; your throne endures to all generations.

9Religion has become weaponized, and worshippers have been killed.
Black Christians were shot inviting a white youth to a Bible class.
10Jews are slaughtered in a synagogue, Mormons in a temple,
Catholic children are shot on the first day of school.
11Mosques are bombed and Muslims are harassed for their faith.
Christ is weeping in his heavens and mothers in their homes.

12There is another shooting in a school; four children and a teacher killed.
Does it matter? It happens all the time; each time our heart grows numb.
13Another shooting in a store, a movie theater, a concert, and a street corner.
Two innocent girls are killed by the spray of bullets from an assault weapon.
14Who will comfort those in their bitter grief, who love their children still;
who will heal the killers' soul; who will stop the sale of guns of war?

15"But guns are necessary," they say, "to keep the bad guys away.
Bad guys are always different; they are not our kind of people.
16Some are brown and others black; others pretend they are smarter than us.
They always want what we have but they will never get it.
17We will defend this society and stuff that is ours,
and, if we get the chance, we will take a little bit of what is theirs."

[18]Britain's politics also are roiled by immigration from commonwealth and rubber boats.
Who will house the immigrants? Why should we pay for their healthcare?
[19]Belarus pushes immigrants across Poland's borders; Russia does the same to Finland.
Is nationalism so fragile it cannot welcome strangers and learn from them?
[20]The civil strife between who we are, and an invading world, is mirrored in every land.
No country can resist this new reality; no weapon can defeat this invasion.

[21]The nations are in an uproar, the kingdoms totter, be still and know that I am God.
I will be exalted among the nations; I am exalted throughout the earth.
[22]As I called Assyria to conquer the nations and Babylon to carry off the treasures of Judah,
can I not bring together the whole world of my making and my redeeming?
[23]Will your little nation survive the onslaught; will it subsist through the strife and conflict?
Then welcome the foreigner, give jobs for the needy, and heal the sick and despairing.

12:3 *Hab 1:3*, **12:5** *Matt 7:3*, **12:6** *Ps 119:157*, **12:7** *Ps 109:3*, **12:8** *Lam 5:1*, **12:11** *Luke 19:41*, **12:14** *Matt 2:18*, **12:21** *Ps 46:5, 10*, **12:23** *Matt 25:35–36*.

Chapter 13

Global Convulsion

[1]Through massive tariffs Trump has disrupted patterns of global trade that have existed for over seventy years. Xi of China displayed an impressive view of military might in front of twenty-six world leaders, especially those of Russia, North Korea, and Iran. China and its allies seek to change the rules-based world order dominated by the United States and replace it with a more imperialist pattern. [2]As the United States itself seeks to dominate both neighbors and allies in a rival imperialist stance, the stage is set for another world war to decide who will set the rules and agenda for the next century.

[3]As in the case of the end of the city states of Israel and Judah replaced by the new imperial systems of Assyria, Babylon, and Persia, the prophets had a different perspective as to the causes of the coming disaster. The focus of their concern was what was happening in Israel and Judah, but their words speak to the whole world today.

[4]While conflicts over migrants and refugees threaten societies
global war kills millions and threatens the future of humanity.
[5]Having ignored and increased the problems of the needy across the world,
there are always funds for the planes, the ships, the drones, and bombs.

[6]But destruction will come first to the powerful nations who have
the weapons of the rich.
Having little left to steal the poorest people may well escape.

[7]What will bring this whirlwind of devastation and the rubble of
our homes?
Will you steal, murder, commit adultery, and make offerings
to Ba'al?
[8]The Ba'al of prosperity has replaced the God of justice in the
hearts of your rulers.
Now prosperity has become the goal of the nation.
[9]On that day I will punish the nations for their transgressions, says
the Lord,
I will tear down their winter house as well as the summer
house.

[10]Are our empires too big to be invaded, invincible in size?
Battles will be fought in neighbor's lands.
[11]Spilling over will be drones and missiles escaping all the shields,
quickening death in quiet places.
[12]Ships will sink, planes will crash, and the young will wait to die.
The bombs of the apocalypse are ready to use.

[13]For these things we weep; the Comforter is too far from us.
Our groans are many; our hearts are faint.
[15]Death has come up into our windows; it has entered our
mansions.
It cuts off our children from the playgrounds, our young men
from the fields.
[16]O God, have you completely rejected your people? Does your
heart loathe America?
Is Russia your target; will you make China poor again, divided
against itself?

[17]Thus says the Lord: Am I not a potter who shapes the future of
the nations?
Can I not cast off the clay for their crimes against my people?
[18]But if those nations, of which I have spoken, turn from their evil
ways,
I will change my mind about the disasters that I intended to
bring on them.
[19]Can I not make wars to cease to the ends of the earth and make
your weapons useless?
Be still and know that I am God; I will be exalted among the
nations, exalted in the earth.
[20]The time is coming when revenge is forgotten, and warring mad-
ness stilled.
They will beat their swords into plowshares and spears into
pruning hooks.
[21]Tariffs will not be used to help ourselves and hurt our neighbors;
trade will be used to provide jobs for the poor and homes for
the homeless.
[22]Migrants, like Ruth, will be welcomed and given homes in
shrinking towns;
their descendants will be a blessing to every nation where they
are welcomed.

13:6 *2 Kgs 25:12*, **13:7** *Jer 7:9*, **13:8** *Jer 11:17*, **13:9** *Amos 3:15*, **13:13** *Lam 1:16, 22*, **13:15** *Jer 9:21*, **13:16** *Jer 14:19*, **13:17** *Jer 18:6–8*, **13:19** *Ps 46:9–10*, **13:20** *Isa 2:4*, **13:22** *Ruth 2:12*.

Chapter 14

A King of the Nations

1Peeking out of a thicket of thorns and toxic weeds grows a wily flower.
Revenge and hatred cannot hold back some deeds of kindness and a touch of love.
2While a nation's rulers quell conflict within and seek victory without,
the King of the nations fights a battle in every human heart
3Is my greatest loyalty, the reason to offer up my life, given to a nation's cause,
or shall I save my sacrifice to serve the cause of the King who has come?

4Would you win the war with cruel disdain for human life,
will you send the fresh-faced youth to meet untimely death?
5God called him before he was born; he was named in his mother's womb.
His sharp sword was the word from his mouth, his presence a polished arrow.
6His weapons do not wound an enemy nor take the life of a father's son.
Rather the sword opens up the conscience so that healing might take place.

7 As soldiers march, tanks rumble down the streets and airplanes fly overhead,
the threat of conflict makes our worries widen and brings numbness to our souls.
8 So different, he had no form of majesty that we might admire, but was despised and rejected.
He was wounded for our transgressions; he was crushed for our iniquities.
9 Yet he will startle many nations and kings will shut their mouths because of him;
forgiveness can create policy, and enemies will be reconciled for peace.

10 Moved by the Spirit, he brings good news to the oppressed and binds up the brokenhearted.
He proclaims liberty to the captives and release of prisoners.
11 While we are dumb in a world of pain he decrees that the Jubilee is here.
He visits vengeance on the selfish and brings comfort for all who mourn.
12 Bring your palms and raise your voices, your King has come.
Blessed is he who comes in the name of the Lord! glory in the highest heaven.

13 But what did he say to the warriors who conquered and killed and nailed him to the cross?
How does he pray for us who are part of injustice, violence, and self-righteousness?
14 "Father, forgive them for they do not know what they are doing."
Dying for the sins and crimes of all, he prays for us as well.
15 Even a thief has hope. "Remember me, a real bummer, in that coming kingdom."
Paradise is there for all who ask, even those who cannot get down from their cross.

16 Darkness invades the sunniest skies and the ground shakes beneath our feet.
With him we cry, "My God, my God, why have you forsaken me?"
17 Hanging there in the cataclysm of God's loathing and love he died.
Teaching us to pray, he said, "Father, into your hands I commend my Spirit."
18 On his cross he was crowned as King of the nations, King of us all.
On our cross we follow him to victory here and beyond.

19 A stony path, an uphill climb, debts must be paid, work finished, death to be faced.
Now the debts have been paid, bad memories erased, he has wiped away all tears.
20 His resurrection has swallowed death and brings to us the victory.
And when our trek is finished, the King welcomes us home.
21 Till then he greets us on the path in the faces of the hungry, the thirsty, and the sick,
and introduces us to migrants, prisoners, and enemies we can love.

14:2 *Jer 10:7,* **14:3** *Luke 9:24,* **14:5** *Isa 49:2,* **14:6** *Heb 4:12,* **14:8** *Isa 53:2–5,* **14:9,** *Isa 52:15,* **14:10** *Luke 4:18, 19,* **14:11** *Lev 25, Isa 61:2,* **14:12** *Luke 19:38,* **14:14** *Luke 23:34,* **14:15** *Luke 23:43,* **14:16** *Matt 27:46,* **14:17** *Luke 23:46,* **14:20** *1 Cor 15:54–56,* **14:21** *Matt 25:35–40.*

Chapter 15

A New World Society

[1]In recent years governments have been overthrown in Madagascar, Nepal, Haiti, Bangladesh, Syria, Tunisia, Libya, Sudan, Sri Lanka, Afghanistan, Myanmar, Burkina Faso, Niger, and Mali. Unrest has plagued many other countries as well. [2]To nations plagued by debt, corruption, climate change, and the unemployment of a growing number of young people, loyalty has grown very thin. While some seek to migrate, others wonder how they can survive in the years to come.

[3]Why do the young face tear gas, water cannons, and well-armed troops?
Will there really be any change should the government fall?
[4]Pregnant, without a future, a young girl sang a song of hope:
"He has put down the mighty from their seats and exalted them of low degree."
[5]An excited old man holds the promised babe and counts his life complete.
Even the unemployed kids in poor nations will see the light revealed.

[6]His first words answered the questions that had been asked across the centuries,
"The Kingdom of God is at hand; repent and believe the good news."

7Growing up in a nation that has failed its people, what is our identity, where our hope?
The Kingdom of God is at hand; it is a whole new world society.
8It is not a room of heaven that is realized here on earth; it is not an undisturbed delight.
It is just the miracle of a child fed, a leper cleansed, and some good news for the poor.

9The money myths have had their say and in many lands have failed us all the way.
Current capitalism does not work in the poorest places of the earth.
10Who will invest in building homes for those in urban slums and refugee camps?
Who will endure the taxation necessary to build the clinics and make schools free?
11When there is already more production of goods than there are funds to buy them,
who will hire the many school leavers looking desperately for money to get married?

12Communism only works when there is wealth to divide and guns to enforce fairness.
Sharing poverty equally leads to stagnation and migration.
13Russia has thrown it off and China turned it inside out.
Cuba struggles but barely survives; North Korea spends food money on missiles.
14Few will fly a Communist flag in demonstrations across the Global South.
Promises unfulfilled have led to failures in finance and hopes deferred.

15How does the Kingdom come; how will a new world society grow?
How can we recognize what God is already doing in our lives?

16Jesus said, "Repent and believe the good news."
Turn away from what you have been doing and look for that which is unbelievably better.
17At that creative moment new possibilities present themselves and fresh horizons open.
There is forgiveness for what you have been doing and hope for the society to come.

18School leavers head to the country to help in agriculture.
The wealthy invest in their own nation instead of Swiss banks.
19Corporations change their practice from exploitation to development.
Governments root out the corruption that cripples the economy.
20They recognize that their greatest wealth is found in their people.
Investing in their food, water, health and learning is their highest priority.

15:4 *Luke 1:52*, **15:5** *Luke 2:29–32*, **15:6** *Mark 1:15*, **15:8** *Luke 4:18*, **15:16** *Mark 1:15*, **1:17** *Luke 19:8–9*.

Chapter 16

Reconciliation of Enemies

1After the end of apartheid in South Africa a Truth and Reconciliation Commission was created to bring about some reconciliation between former enemies. Victims of violence on both sides were invited to tell their stories. If those who caused the violence told the truth about their involvement and asked for forgiveness, they
were given amnesty. 2Since then, Truth and Reconciliation Commissions have been set up in Canada, Northern Ireland, Columbia, Sierra Leone, and elsewhere.

3Why is it a sin to kill a man and then have to face his family in court?
The punishment for murder is death or life in prison.
4Why is it easy to kill thousands in war, face no blame, and come back a hero?
But never forget, the families of the fallen will plot revenge and murder.
5Forgiven by Christ a mother will forgive her son's murderer
but how can a whole stricken people make peace with their oppressors and killers?

6Come, let us argue it out; though your sins are as scarlet, they shall be white as snow.
But what will you do with that forgiveness in an unforgiving world?

7How do you make peace with someone who seeks to destroy you and yours?
Forgiveness has a hard time of it in the midst of war.
8Lord, is this why your good news comes after the destruction that has brought us low?
Will defeat bring us to the repentance that brings reconciliation?

9After the war Germans and French work together to build a new Europe.
Blacks and whites struggle together to build South Africa.
10But might we seek harmony and peace without our mutual ruin?
Can Canada make peace with its indigenous people?
11Its colonists now repent for ripping children from their parent's arms.
The church has apologized for the rape and abuse and murder of kids.

12Come, let us argue it out. Is an apology enough; is forgiveness the end?
Many of the wounded want compensation for the injuries suffered.
13Though your sins are red like crimson, they shall be white as wool.
But if you are not obedient and practice justice you will be devoured.
14Are our princes rebels and companions of thieves to run after gifts?
Must they not rather defend the orphan and widow and help the addict?

15When a truth teller condemns violence and murder and is thrown into a pit,
he prays that God would not forgive their iniquity; there will be no forgiveness for them.

[16]But when a whole nation has suffered because of their crimes and injustice,
God relents and promises full forgiveness for all of their iniquity.
[17]God's mercy is great and forgives the multitude of transgressions.
But be not so confident of forgiveness that you add sin to sin.

[18]While nations boast of their powers and parade their weapons of war,
forgiveness does not even appear on their radar,
[19]but when little is left but rubble in the streets and pictures of dead on the wall,
the injured will live in a world of wounded enemies.
[20]In my anguish I sent my Son to die, that sinners might be forgiven, enemies reconciled.
The resurrection brings new life to the dead and a better hope for peace.

16:5 *Matt 6:15,* **16:6** *Isa 1:18,* **16:7** *Isa 2:9,* **16:12** *Isa 1:18–20,* **16:14** *Isa 1:23,* **16:15** *Jer 18:23,* **16:16** *Jer 33:8,* **16:17** *Sir 5:5, Rom 6:1–2,***16:20** *Rom 5:8, Col 1:20.*

Chapter 17

Food for All

1In the besieged city the famine was so severe there was no food
for the people.
Jerusalem starved under Nebuchadnezzar, Gaza under
Netanyahu.
2Oppressors always use hunger as a weapon of war.
See the bones and sunken eyes of captives and mothers without food.
3Forgotten in the conflicts in Sudan, Somalia, the Congo, Haiti,
and Afghanistan,
the children beg for food, and no one gives them anything.

4When there is no rain the corn and beans fail to grow. How shall
we live?
None will lend us money anymore; food costs too much.
5The floods have swept away the spring plantings; water has never
been so deep.
Escaping with our lives, what will we eat in the year to come?
6Who has permitted the climate to change; who will continue to let
the poor suffer?
Has our God gone to sleep? Will our prayers wake him up to
bring us food?

7The eyes of all wait upon you, O Lord, and you give them food in due season.
The Lord of Hosts will make for all peoples a feast of rich food.
8Food trucks will arrive, flour for bread, peanut paste for the kids will come.
Just a partial payment for all the pain and wounds of war.
9But peace will come, and I will bring it as I have always done,
and they will be radiant over the goodness of the Lord, the grain, the wine and the oil.

10As Jesus fed thousands we are feeding tens of thousands everywhere.
His disciples work in food banks and refugee camps.
11Grocery clerks put their extra food in boxes for those out of work.
Postmen pick up groceries for everyone's Thanksgiving.
12Without any dirt on our hands, and without shovel or rake,
we can still write a check with care from our hearts and prayer from our lips.

13Lasting ways to supply food and the greedy are being explored and found.
Food vouchers help the poor buy food from local farmers who can produce more.
14Climate-smart agriculture grows crops in well-watered fields.
Plants requiring little water are growing in drought-affected places.
15Sun-dried food can be stored for those times when food is scarce.
They prepare food in summer and gather its substance at harvest.

16In Africa's cities boys without work should go back to the country to farm.
Who tills the land will have plenty of bread, but who follows worthless pursuits will have plenty of poverty.

[17]Mothers receive education to supply good nutrition to their families.
They also need the power to gain access to food and be providers for their children.
[18]Communities can join together to share solutions for their lack of food.
To a threatened people the Lord says: Assemble yourselves and come together and draw near to survive.

[19]As long as the earth endures, seedtime and harvest, cold and heat, summer and winter, day and night shall not cease.
There is enough food on earth for all to eat.
[20]God will feed his flock like a shepherd and gather the lambs in his arms;
all will feed along the ways and even bad land will be a pasture.
[21]Warmed by his promises, moved by his Spirit, we are called to help.
When feeding a hungry child Jesus says, "You have done it unto me."

17:1 *Jer 52:6*, **17:3** *Lam 4:4*, **17:6** *Ps 31:24*, **16:7** *Ps 145:15*, *Isa 25:6*, **17:9** *Jer 31:12*, **17:15** *Prov 6:8* **17:18** *Isa 45:20*, **17:19** *Gen 8:22*, **17:20** *Isa 40:11*, *49:9*, **17:21** *Matt 25:35*.

Chapter 18

Water for the World

1"Send us rain," they pray in the parched lands across the world.
A farmer looks to heaven in the third year of drought.
2Without water cattle die and the sun dries out their bones.
The corn dies in the field, the beans are gone, disaster is near.
3Has God commanded that no rain fall upon the land because of our iniquity?
Have we changed the climate with the worship of false gods?

4Flexing their muscles, deserts are growing where people need to live.
Streams have stopped flowing; the wells are almost empty.
5Irrigation holds promises of plenty if reservoirs receive their flow,
but burgeoning cities need their share for washing and waste.
6Downstream little is left but moist sand and damaged dreams.
Will wars over water replace the struggles over land?

7Yet in pleasant places the rains do not stop but hurry to destroy.
Floods sweep all away and the torrent rages over us.
8Like an army of enemy forces, the land is invaded by ruin and death.
Like creeping despair, the waters come up to our necks.
9We wait for the dove to come back with an olive leaf to show the water's gone.
Till then we must build our collective house upon the rock.

10The floods avoid the desert land, the shifting sand, the drifting dunes.
But the sun enjoys his liberties as he bakes the broken land.
11The Lord speaks to the traveler crossing the wilderness gone dry.
He shouts good news to the keeper of the cattle and tender of the garden.
12The wilderness and the dry land will be glad and will blossom abundantly.
The crocus will rejoice with joy and singing.

13I will open rivers on the bare heights, and fountains in the valleys.
I will make the wilderness a pool of water and springs of water in the dry land.
14I will pour water on the thirsty lands and streams on the dry ground.
Your offspring will spring up like trees, like willows by flowing streams.
15Can these promises which brought Israel to their home come true again?
Can the wastelands be watered so that all life there is worth living?

16With hand-dug wells, help is available to shatter the rock met halfway down.
The young can lift up the pails of rock and dirt.
17Tube wells are more accurate now and can find water nearly all the time.
Villagers can drink the water and take some home for Mom.
18Plastic sheets line the dugout reservoirs to hold the rain for the dry times.
Fences keep out the wildlife long enough to use the water for cooking.

19If Jews and Arabs work together building solar fields in sun baked lands,
the power to pipe ocean's processed waters to dry lands will be here.

20New land will be opened for grazing and farming.
Moisture will be lifted up to create clouds pregnant with rain.
21Trees and grass will swallow some of the sun's rays.
And maybe we will live on a cooler world.

18:3 *Isa 5:6, Jer 3:2–3,* **18:7** *Ps 124:3–4,* **18:8** *Ps 69:1–2,* **18:9** *Gen 8:11, Luke 6:48,* **18:12** *Isa 35:1–2,* **18:13** *Isa 41:18,* **18:14** *Isa 44:3–4.*

Chapter 19

When Healing Is Free

1 Which are the illnesses that people notice most?
Those that divide people from each other and the community.
2 Feeling cursed are the blind, the deaf, being a cripple and worst of all, being a leper.
Cure for these means a special welcome from those we love.
3 Worst of all are those that cause quick death as with the serpent's sting.
Moses lifts the brass serpent and looking to it, the dying are healed.

4 Freely I will heal the blind by a road they do not know; I will guide them;
I will turn the darkness before them into light, says the Lord.
5 Then the eyes of the blind will be opened, the ears of the deaf unstopped.
Then the lame shall leap like the deer and the tongue of the speechless sing for joy.
6 Even when some are sick through their sinful ways and cry to the Lord,
I will heal them and save them from destruction.

7 A promise is but a seed too small to notice;
who can tell of what it may become?

8It flowered when Jesus chose to cleanse a leper
and healed Peter's mother-in-law so she could serve supper.
9Then it blossomed as Jesus gave sight to the blind, and hearing to the deaf.
The paralyzed walked, the dumb could speak, and just touching his garment brought healing.

10Like a dandelion at the point of death the seeds of healing were blown afar.
Disciples commanded and raised up the lame to walk.
11The sick were laid out on cots so that Peter's shadow would fall on them.
A great number to the disciples came and were cured.
12What joy there was for a man called Aeneas.
Paralyzed for eight long years, he was healed by Peter.

13Seeds flying further, monasteries provided compassion for the ill.
Like Luke, Christian physicians attended to hundreds more.
14Named after Bethlehem, hospitals treated the mentally ill.
Sisters devoted their entire lives for their care.
15Clinics were created for the care of the suffering in the far places of the world.
Just like Jesus, they treated the poor for free.

16Now Providence, Good Samaritan, Immanuel, Franciscan name the hospitals,
but millions are needed to fund the care of their patients.
17Patients can go bankrupt as doctors become wealthy;
makers of drugs and medical supplies swallow patient's savings.
18Must children undergoing cancer treatment pay for the advertising of drugs?
Must premiums for health insurance push a family into poverty?

18 As Jesus and his disciples healed freely, as missionary clinics served the poor,
might the promises of the prophets inspire free healthcare for the needy?
19 Free medical education can provide more doctors for the unserved people of the world.
It will also reduce the money needed to pay for a physician's help.
20 With many more physicians, limited drug advertising, and care moved by compassion,
we can have a less expensive system; we can have Medicare for all.

19:3 *Num 21:8,* **19:4** *Isa 42:16,* **19:5** *Isa 35:5–6,* **19:6** *Ps 107:14–20,* **19:8** *Matt 8:2–3, 14–15,* **19:9** *Matt 15:31, Mark 7:32–35, 37, Luke 8:47,* **19:11** *Acts 5:15–16,* **19:12** *Acts 9:33–34.*

Chapter 20

Jobs and Housing

1The lion is lost; where shall it turn? His appetite is gone; his teeth have rotted.
The world's poor are a mighty beast that does not know how to hunt.
2Communism is a flickering flame that fails to light the way.
Socialism struggles to find jobs and housing in poverty's world.
3Building better housing for slum dwellers has never been the capitalist plan;
cutting down labor costs has not produced jobs for the unemployed.

4Imprisoned in a system not of their own making the poor hear great news.
"They will all sit under their own vines and fig trees."
5Memories are stirred of Israel's early days where every family had land.
Each one had a place to call home and a job to work the land that was their own.
6When greed created riches and sloth and sickness made people sell their land and daughters,
I created the Jubilee that land might be returned, and slaves released.

7Jubilee today might be an international labor pool of recognized and welcomed workers.
Nations will apply for them to pick their crops, do their science, and care for their kids.
8After seven years of honest and good labor they will be received as citizens of their new nation.
Their children will compete in sports with everyone else.
9Like salt and spice they will bring new life to cultures that have grown stale.
Intercultural societies will live at peace with their international neighbors.

10What people in ancient days gave land to the poor and freedom for slaves?
Seek them out if you can find them. There is not one.
11Which of the handmade gods ever commanded their people to rest?
No money might be made on the Sabbath. Take a year off to stay human.
12Make no profit off of the poverty of your neighbor.
Charge no interest when you loan money to those in need.

13Jesus announced good news for the poor when he said the Jubilee is here.
The poor will receive jobs they can control and homes they can live in.
14Employees will own the firm or will be 51 percent of the boards of control.
Companies will make the goods that people need to stay alive and thrive.
15No longer will success be measured by the amount of profit produced
but by how people can create a better life for themselves and their children.

16Ba'al's prophets did not like the Sabbath and the Jubilee then or now.
The Jubilee failed and the destruction of the nation was not far behind.
17It was not efficient enough to produce the prosperity that everyone wanted.
It did not allow the freedom people sought to make more for themselves.
18Selfishness makes the world go around; greed is here to stay; it is even "Christian"
until the destroyer comes and takes it all away.

19Then there will be work for all to clean up the rubble and use it to build homes.
Those who work with their hands will be the leaders.
20All will decide how to order the society so that all can survive;
all will be free to dream, and plan, and labor for what comes next.
21If they call upon me I will be there to help them to work and to rest.
I will feed them with good things and will call them all my children.

20:4 *Mic 4:4, Zech 3:10,* **20:5** *Num 26:52–56,* **20:6** *Lev 25,* **20:11** *Ps 116:7, Lev 25:4,* **20:13** *Luke 4:21,* **20:21** *Ps 5:15, Mic 5:4.*

Chapter 21

Freedom for Captives

1When Spartacus led the slave rebellion, it was extinguished.
The roads to Rome were decorated with the crucified captives.
2When I liberated the Hebrew slaves from Egypt
their royal pursuers were lost in the waters of the sea.
3That story is told in prisons and by slaves around the world.
"How long, O Lord, before you liberate us?"

4The Lord executes justice for the oppressed; he gives food to the hungry.
The Lord sets the prisoners free.
5Who can count the prisoners in Israeli jails who fought to save their land?
How many immigrants are in US jails awaiting deportation?
6Exodus was the battle hymn of the poor in Latin America.
Their cries stirred the church to proclaim that God was on their side.

7Women in Afghanistan cannot leave the house to learn and work.
Their slavery is justified by a faith turned upside down.
8Fishing boats have captured youth to fish without wages.
The pimps of prostitutes will not let them go free.
9Nigerian girls and boys are captured by Boko Haram;
torture, beatings, and abuse threaten their lives.

10As Jesus' land was ruled by Roman legions,
whole nations struggle under conquest.
11Corrupt governments steal from their people,
they murder and imprison all who would defy them.
12When will you use a mighty Cyrus to set your people free?
When will our Nehemiah help us rebuild again?

13You gave Joseph the power to interpret dreams to set him free.
You moved the world to release Mandela as he forgave his enemies.
14Colonies were liberated from those who would exploit them.
You delivered Eastern Europe from Communist oppression.
15How long, O Lord, slaves and prisoners wait for your power to free;
give all the patience to wait for your liberation.

16Fearing crime, offenders face a vengeful public.
Politicians get votes promising longer sentences.
17Where can prisoners gain the skills to compete in a world that does not care?
Will repentance be enough to find a job to feed a family?
18No one wants a halfway house in their neighborhood.
Who will wait for an addict to find a cure when he does not have a home?

19I provided whole cities of refuge for those guilty of manslaughter.
They were in the cities of the Levites, parsonages for the outcasts.
20Hundreds of ghost towns dot the states and regions of the land.
Isolated, they are not in anyone's backyard.
21What wonderful cities of refuge these might make for many offenders
raising crops and cattle, building homes, enforcing laws, and learning love.

[22]What is it like to be a slave who must serve another and lose all initiative?
We do all in our power to be free and stay out of prison.
[23]But freedom is a fantasy when we are slaves to our own impulses.
We are prisoners of our prejudices and locked into our own affections.
[24]With joy we hear, "Christ has proclaimed liberty to the captives.
If the Son has made you free, you will be free indeed."

21:2 *Exod 15:19*, **21:4** *Ps 146:7*, **21:12** *Isa 45:13*, **21:13** *Gen 41:35*, **21:15** *Ps 119:84*, **21:19** *Num 35:6*, **21:23** *John 8:34*, **21:24** *John 8:36*.

Chapter 22

Ending Wars

1How do you speak to a soldier who has lost a limb?
What do you say to a mother who has lost her son?
2We are assaulted by the body bags in Gaza, especially those of children.
We look away from the pictures of dead soldiers on a wall in Kiev.
3Do not even mention the massacres in the Sudan.
Forget about all that as we must prepare for supper.

4Our minds turn off the images of war; we do not want to look.
Our ears can no longer hear the cries for help.
5Numbness has gripped the world and will not let go.
We are too used to tragedy to care about another conflict.
6Is this why a returning soldier cannot sleep at night?
Last week one of his buddies took his life.

7Shattering the numbness is the gift of tears.
Jeremiah weeps a fountain of tears for the slain.
8Jesus wept over the coming destruction of Jerusalem;
God cried over the siege, the famine and the killing.
9What good are a few tears in the face of overwhelming sadness?
The weeping mothers of Gaza have changed the world.

10Who made up the doctrine that when your nation is attacked it must retaliate?
Is vengeance one of the "must do" commandments of international politics?
11Is this why the cemeteries of fallen soldiers have such terrible beauty?
The neat rows conceal the agony of too many young men who died way too soon.
12Why is war always that "tragic" necessity—"Nothing else will work"?
Why must children pay the price for incompetent statesmen?

13How can you make selfishness look like a laudable virtue
and greed a value worth fighting for?
14Patriotism is a wonderful excuse for wars of exploitation.
Even defending what we have is worth a battle.
15Is God on the side of the enemy to punish the crimes of our citizens?
Are our sins against the migrant and the vulnerable the real cause of war?

16The nations are in an uproar, the kingdoms totter; he utters his voice, the earth melts.
We hear the sound of the trumpet, the alarm of war.
17Where can we hide? Will our nation be our savior?
But what if our nation is the enemy and God is on the other side?
18Our anguish may soon be like that of the returning soldier.
No one understands that war makes us writhe in pain.

19The Lord of Hosts is with us; God is our refuge; he makes wars to cease.
He breaks the bow and shatters the spear.
20Every war has its ending, some in victory, others in compromise.
We pray that God may hurry them to come sooner.

[21]We long to beat swords into plowshares and spears into pruning
hooks,
when nations live at peace and learn war no more.

22:7 *Jer 9:1,* **22:8** *Luke 19:41,* **22:15** *Jer 22:3–9,* **22:16** *Ps 46:6, Jer 4:19,* **22:17** *Jer 27:6,* **22:18** *Jer 4:19,* **22:19** *Ps 46:7–9,* **22:21** *Isa 2:4, Mic 4:3.*

Chapter 23

Forgiveness, Repentance and Forgiveness

[1]Forgiveness is an open invitation to repent.
Though your sins be as scarlet, they shall be white as snow.
[2]What an introduction to the heady list of sins that were to follow.
Sins that caused the death of a nation and end of an era.
[3]Wounded for our transgressions, bruised for our iniquities,
the chastisement of our peace was upon him and by his stripes we are healed.

[4]Come, let us argue it out; you leaders will do everything to gain and keep wealth.
You do not defend the disabled, heal the addicted, or aid the homeless.
[5]I will enter into judgment with the powerful in government and business.
You have devoured the wages of workers and the pensions of the poor.
[6]What do you mean by crushing my people and grinding the faces of the needy?
How do you feel about deporting fathers and orphaning their children?

7You join house to house and field to field until there is room for no one but you.
Have I not sworn that many beautiful houses will be desolate without inhabitants?
8Why do you call evil good and good evil, darkness for light and light for darkness?
Ah, you are wise in your own eyes and shrewd in your own sight.
9You are sowing thistles and weeds in a good field of growing wheat.
They will all be gathered in the days of judgment you will face.

10It is hard to repent, to tell yourself what you have done is wrong.
Your rationales were fake; your beliefs were crooked.
11But it is even harder to believe the good news.
Your sins are forgiven, and you are one of God's friends.
12Jesus has died and risen again that you might again have a clean conscience,
not because of the good you have done but because of what he did for you.

13The Kingdom of God is near, Jesus said, with forgiveness and blessings.
As you repent of the sins that devastate others and change your ways
14then believe the good news that, as new people, the poor will eat;
that there will be homes for the homeless and healing for the sick.
15Say goodbye to cynicism and embrace the hope that brings new energy to your life.
Stand with the suffering and rejoice in a new life of hope and vigor.

16In Christ we have redemption through his blood, the forgiveness of our trespasses,
according to the riches of his grace which he lavished upon us.

17 Dimly peering into the future, we begin to understand the very mystery of life.
His plan is to gather up all things to himself, things in heaven and on earth.
18 In him the whole purpose of life is not to hate, to polarize, and to divide,
but as a hen gathers her chicks let Christ bring us together to love one another.

23:1 *Isa 1:18*, **23:3** *Isa 53:5*, **23:4** *Isa 3:13–24*, **23:7** *Isa 5:8–9*, **23:8** *Isa 5:20–21*, **23:9** *Matt 13:25–30*, **23:12** *Heb 10:22*, *Rom 3:28*, **23:13, 14** *Mark 1:15*, **23:16** *Eph 1:7–8*, **23:17** *Eph 1:9–10*, **23:18** *Matt 23:37*.

Chapter 24

The End of Death

1Like the sun breaking through the cloudy skies
  are the promises of God in terrible times.
2We will exalt our God who does wondrous things.
  Ruthless enemies are denied their place of refuge.
3When those in conflict face famine and the death of children,
  the Lord of Hosts will provide a feast for all.

4The shroud of death hangs over every battlefield
  and invades the hospice and hospitals.
5The fear of death is never far away and haunts the stoutest hearts.
  It challenges our hopes and erects a ceiling on the future.
6But into the gloom shouts God's startling promise:
  God will swallow up death forever.

7Then the Lord will wipe away every tear from our eyes
  as he transforms our fear of death into new life.
8"Rum thing," the skeptic said. "It looks like Jesus really rose from the dead."
  From the catacombs comes the chant, "Christ is arisen."
9Awake my heart with gladness; see what new life can mean.
  Hopes are renewed and the future's ceiling is gone.

10With death swallowed and resurrection promised, how shall we live?
An aging president worries over what will come next.
11Putin and Xi speculate whether life might be extended further;
they mourn the loss of all their power in the life to come.
12They will be as weak as their lowliest subject.
The rich will have no more than the poor they exploited.

13Unafraid of death there is courage to do what's right.
There is an unbelievable bravery to confront what's evil.
14The path ahead is lit with the glow of the mansions to be ours.
Christ prepared them for all those longing for a real home.
15Join hands with those who are losing their way.
Let your joy be seen and your love be felt.

16Like a bride waiting for her groom to come
we wait with well-lit lamps full of oil.
17Though delayed we keep each other company.
His Spirit warms us as we imagine joys to come.
18Little did we know back then when we thought of death,
it will be the wondrous wedding day with our beloved.

24:2 *Isa 25:2,* **24:3** *Isa 25:6,* **24:6** *Isa 25:8,* **24:7** *Isa 25:8,* **24:8** *1 Cor 15:4,* **24:10** *1 Cor 15:58,* **24:14** *John 14:1–3,* **24:16** *Matt 25:4.*

Chapter 25

Thy Kingdom Come

1Lord of the nations, have mercy on us for thinking our nation is your Kingdom.
"Make America Great Again" is not part of the prayer your taught us.
2Announcing your Kingdom, you healed the sick and fed the hungry.
America has cut their aid to AIDS patients and starving infants.
3You called on us to welcome refugees like Mary, Joseph and Jesus.
The president announced no more refugees from the poorest nations.

4Like a blaze out of control, a new religion has ignited a political firestorm;
calling itself Christian it denies what Christ has taught about love.
5With righteous anger, it condemns those who welcome and defend the stranger.
It turns a blind eye to the cruelties of those they elected.
6The Christians they praise and remember with godly piety are mostly white.
They exclude the colored masses their own missionaries sought to save.

7 Must one learn the Word of God to call oneself a Christian in the culture war?
Can you not learn more from the Christians in the president's cabinet?
8 Yet the Word of God is like a two-edged sword that cuts apart the lies
and will devour the ties that bind political power with a false faith.
9 From the beginning that Word created the whole world in which we live
and was preached to people of all colors and nations for their good.

10 The Kingdom of God is found throughout the whole world.
It is embraced by a multicolored pallet of people.
11 Their patriotism is to the Lord who bought them with a price.
His cross is the flag they wear and honor.
12 They trace their history and their destiny through the ages.
They honor martyrs who give up their lives for their faith.

13 Would you honor your nation, the land in which you live?
Then let it be like the mountain of the Lord.
14 Let it be a place where the Word of the Lord is taught and practiced
not only by the poor but also by the powerful.
15 Let it arbitrate and make peace between nations.
Keep it from all wars of choice.

16 As it again follows the rule of law, and practices fairness,
it will continue to be a safe place to live.
17 It will build more houses for the homeless and the refugee
and give all an opportunity to work and thrive.
18 Then thousands more will seek to learn what makes this nation great
and return home to teach the lessons they have learned.

[19]How does the Kingdom come to our nation and the world?
Silly thought! It comes like a sower throwing seed.
[20]Results take time and they are only partial, but we are impatient
and grow discouraged, ready to give up.
[21]But when every nation fails, and they will,
God's will be the last Kingdom standing; hope in a world of
crisis.

25:1 *Ps 33:10, Matt 6:9–13*, **25:2** *Mark 1:15, 34*, **25:3** *Matt 25:35*, **25:8** *Isa 49:2, Matt 10:34*, **25:9** *John 1:3*, **25:11** *1 Cor 6:20*, **25:13** *Isa 2:2–3*, **25:15** *Isa 2:4*, **25:19** *Matt 13:18–23*, **25:21** *Dan 2:44*.

www.ingramcontent.com/pod-product-compliance
Lightning Source LLC
LaVergne TN
LVHW020654100826
845148LV00012B/2490

* 9 7 9 8 3 8 5 2 7 4 7 7 2 *